THE
WARRIOR

RYAN GARDNER

The Warrior
Copyright © 2021 by Ryan Gardner

All rights reserved. No part of this publication may be reproduced, distributed, or transmitted in any form or by any means, including photocopying, recording, or other electronic or mechanical methods, without the prior written permission of the author, except in the case of brief quotations embodied in critical reviews and certain other non-commercial uses permitted by copyright law.

tellwell

Tellwell Talent
www.tellwell.ca

ISBN
978-0-2288-6043-3 (Hardcover)
978-0-2288-6042-6 (Paperback)
978-0-2288-6044-0 (eBook)

**for anyone fighting their own battle
whatever that battle may be**

stay strong.

SWEET SIXTEEN

Every dream was similar, usually starting off in a sweet paradise, feeling happy and at peace. I remember running and playing, never stopping to appreciate my beautiful surroundings or - if there were others - appreciating their kindness. In a flash, the dream would change; the ending always the same.

A feeling of dread would wash over me as the sky turned from blue to grey. The ground below changed from soft soil to sharp needles, jabbing into the soles of my feet, ensuring I could not run. The wind became cold, and as I looked down the path in front of me, my heart drops into my stomach. A tall, dark shadow began to slowly walk towards me. I could not run so instead, I screamed - I roared! - hoping to scare it away. Before I could see its face, I would wake up in panic. My sheets were drenched in sweat, skin moist and hot. I shivered in a cold sweat, finding the blanket trying to fall back to sleep.

This happened every night.

As things became progressively worse, visits to the family doctor became more frequent. Mom and I walked into the doctor's office for our weekly appointment, ready to repeat my symptoms to our doctor (again). By this point, I couldn't run, or walk up stairs without coughing up a lung, often causing me to get sick. I was losing weight at an alarming rate. My hair became thinner; my skin dull and grey. I slept constantly, usually only waking up to go to school and eat dinner. It was frustrating: we seemed to be getting nowhere.

However, this appointment was different. Another doctor walked through the doors and called my name. As we walked towards the scale, she explained that our regular physician was on vacation so she would be our doctor for the day.

We began to explain my symptoms, noting that the last "solution" prescribed - a nasal spray - was ineffective. The doctor nodded as she read through my files, eyes fixed in deep concentration. She seemed puzzled, flipping through each document, getting more and more frustrated.

After a few minutes, she closed the folder, and set it on her desk. The room was silent for a few moments before the doctor looked up, letting out a sigh.

"I think you should get an x-ray."

*

Mom and I were silent as we drove back from the x-ray, my mind racing in worry. As we pulled into the driveway, Mom put the car in park and turned to me. Her eyes were wide with worry.

"What is going on with you?"

"I don't know, Mom," the first tear rolling slowly down my cheek.

" I don't know."

*

"Ryan?"

My parents and I followed the doctor into a small office. A box full of toys, crayons and a child's art sat in the corner. Three chairs sat at the opposite end of a large, wooden desk. They sat down.

The doctor took a sigh, looking at each of them with sad eyes before the ball was dropped.

"Ryan, you have Hodgkins Lymphoma - stage 2 (B) due to the size of your tumors. There is one sitting in your collarbone that's the size of a large grape. The second is the size of a grapefruit and has been pressing on your lungs - it's most likely the reason you've had so much trouble breathing."

He continued to explain the treatment plan: chemotherapy and radiation. Mom and Dad both hugged me as they cried. I was in a state of shock and didn't understand what he was telling me.

I'm supposed to go on a trip next week... Surely, I would be able to go...right?

The doctor's face became sadder as I asked the question, looking me in the eye to tell me I couldn't go.
My parents hugged me harder as I started to sob.

cancer

hello, see your encompassed by fear
the war starts today
so sad that you ended up here
all fighting no time to play

we're going to try
we're going to fight
the large tumours living
on your insides

we'll search for a cure
but forget who you were
for now you are
a warrior

grumble

morning doctor!
what's the plan?

"we're going to cut you open my friend!
we don't have a time - no, not yet...but don't you worry!
you can fill your tummy soon.
just drink your water, and
everything will be
just fine"

afternoon, doctor!
any word on the time yet?

"sorry, hunny, and i'm not quite sure why.
i'll call down to the surgeon-
she might have an answer..
i know you're hungry,
i know you're stressed.

you'll go down soon
be patient and
i promise
everything will be
just fine."

evening, doctor!
it's getting kind of late...do we-

"time to get ready - you're going down for 8!

get into your gown,
i'll give you the rundown:
you won't be put under,
just some painkillers for you.

it should only take an hour or two.
don't worry,
you won't feel a thing!
everything will be
just fine.

"and best of all,
dinner's on its way!"

tummy grumbles happily,
for soon there will be food.

metal tree

let me roam,
smile at the little warriors in the hallways
push myself forward

let me laugh,
spend time with family and friends
focus on those moments when times are tough

let me speak,
tell my story,
inspire others to cross the finish line

let me be strong,
always remember
slow and steady wins the race

teddy bear

Very late one evening
I heard a little girl crying
Confused tears; her mother
Trying to calm her down - both of them so scared.
Open the curtain, smile and hand her a teddy bear
Ryan is my name; I know you're scared but,
I'll promise you one thing, my friend - it will be
All right.

"Now sleep, little warrior, it's time to say goodnight."

remind yourself

you are brave
you are beautiful
you are smart
you are funny
you are wise
you are strong

forever young

take a breathe
one (smile)
two (cry)
three (run)
not away from your woes but,
towards your goals
breathe in and (exhale)
peace of mind

THE SCARE

We walked down the hallways of Sick Kids McMaster hospital with smiles on our faces. Everything seemed fine. I was back at school getting good grades; reunited with old friends and making new ones too. Life seemed to be back to normal. We were happy. The illness that took away the summer before seemed like a distant nightmare. It was over and we could move forward. Little did we know that the appointment that lay ahead was going to squash that.

After a long wait in the room filled with sick children we were called into a smaller one, ready to get the usual news: everything was A-okay and to keep up the good work. Unfortunately, that wasn't what we got. We were shocked for I wasn't part of the ninety percent of patients that were cured after the treatment. The Hodgkins had returned. A CT scan showed a lymph node in my left armpit was swollen and that meant the cancer was back.

The doctors then told us what would come next. It was November and since my eighteenth birthday was just months away, I would be transferred to Juravinski Cancer Centre - a clinic beside the hospital where I would be treated. It was scary. I thought the first battle would be the last. We drove home in so sad. Why me?

In the coming days, we would meet our new oncologist - Dr. Foley. Mom had found a naturopathic treatment called "The Gerson Therapy" which included organic, cold-pressed juicing that was said to have the ability to cleanse the cancer out. Foley scheduled a CT scan two months after meeting us, giving us time to try it out. I juiced everyday and guess what?

It worked.

welcome to adulthood

hello, pleased to meet ya
you must be afraid
see your mamma did her research
see you feel the same

you've got some time,
a couple months or so
been a year but
we have it under control

confident this'll work
book a CT to be sure
its game time,
young warrior.

drink your fruits and veggies!

all day everyday
curing disease the healthy way
greens and carrots and apples for days
need 20 lbs of greens?
let me show you the way

juice juice juice,
for breakfast, for lunch
the clock has ticked
its the end of the month

let's do the scan
get the results
no matter what happens
no one's at fault

the phone rings later
i was hoping it would!
"you're all cleared! you're fine!
you're all good!"

hooray, hoorah!
this is wonderful news!
no more juice for me,
now, let's hit up that drive-thru

park life forever

weaving through route 60
taking in the army of emerald giants guarding the animals
living amongst them
art is all around us
inhaling sweet scents

sun and clouds work together to create an abstract masterpiece
slowly becoming darker
a full moon appearing as bright stars begin to sparkle across the dark sky

faces illuminated by warm flames
the final night of summer season brings
laughter
the morning after brings tears
chaos as some move forward into the fall

walk outside the new staff house
enjoying a warm, black coffee,
taking in the beauty of the world outside
a plethora of flames splattered upon
a canvas of blue or grey
ready to brighten the day

ashes spread upon the ground feeding
the ever-changing giants
forever standing tall
ready to be reborn

chopped down to recreate
red, yellow, orange

take a sip and remember
this is home

sticks and stones

sticks and stones
may break my bones
and your words
can still hurt me

tumor

regretting
the burgers
the fries
the chocolate
the candy
the pop
the alcohol
ashamed.

forgetting
the happy days
the good times
the smiles
the laughs
the hikes
the canoe trips
depressed.

dreading
the diagnosis
the biopsy
the treatment
the needles
the drugs,
the pills
fearful.

helpless

i'd rather be dead a lot of the time. i dream of floating away; away from all my problems to a place where no one knows my name. i dream of a new beginning where i don't allow myself to hurt or hurt others. i sometimes wish for a world where greed does not exist and selfishness is not apparent. i don't know what to do anymore.

i feel so unbelievably helpless.

LOST

I am lying on the white tiles of the bathroom floor. Time passes by so slowly as my discomfort grows with every minute. *Jesus Christ* plays through my headphones as tears stained with mascara drip down onto the floor below.

I think of Death frequently now, of her inevitability, her beauty. As Heidegger once said, death is the only thing we know for sure. In a world filled with so many opinions of the afterlife - a debate over the way we must live to be granted access to euphoria - we all can agree that one day, we will die. The possibility of facing that day no longer scared me. Instead, I felt immense self hatred for how little I had achieved, how little I had seen. It was unbearable.

Do you believe you're missing out;
That everything good is happening somewhere else?

It had been one month since my diagnosis. My family were the only ones around, with the exception of the painters and construction workers that frequented the house. I had no friends; no one to call, no one to text. I thought back to the first summer in Algonquin; the nights spent on the bridge outside Mew Lake Campground as we stared up at the constellations and stars dusted across the inky sky.

I thought of the hikes, the exhilaration of getting to the top of a lookout, each tree painted so carefully on the blue canvas, each cloud strolling through the sky lazily as the breeze tickled my ears, sending shivers down my spine.

I thought of the laughs we shared in the Annex; walking down to the campfire on Canada Day empty handed; Gill handing me a beer, the early beginnings of our friendship; the time Traci got so high that all she could say was "Yo"; the final staff party where I teared up knowing that most of the amazing people I had met would be going home, never to be seen again.

I remember as summer turned to autumn, the canvas now filled with reds, yellows and oranges as Gill and I moved into our new home. I clung to these memories of freedom; clung to the idea that I would one day be as happy as I was that summer. But for now, I waited.

Well, Jesus Christ, I'm alone again,
So, what did you do those three days you were dead?
'Cause this problem's going to last...more than the weekend

I sobbed quietly because it was true. The months ahead would be filled with wasted time, moping around waiting for the end. It was agonizing when my mind would wander into an anxious frenzy of possibilities. All the wasted time spent driving to McDonald's or Wendy's, all the opportunities I had wasted due to my lack of confidence, motivation and drive, all the friends lost, the time ahead that would be ripped from me. I realize now my biggest fear is lost time - a realization I wish I had discovered three years prior.

And I will die all alone
And when I arrive...I won't know anyone

I would be surrounded by Death, hear her cries and pleading victims. I would see her face, the darkness that encircled the red, glassy eyes, her open mouth spilling out silent sobs, cheeks stained with dark tear tracks. Perhaps she would snatch my soul up as I slept in a drug induced coma, leaving only my body as proof that I had ever existed.

I thought of the many ways in which she would approach me, thought of the various possibilities in which she could help me escape if my worn-out body failed me, of the ways I could initiate a meeting. That is how I passed the time when my distractions became tired and boring, when I was forced to lie on the cold ceramic tiles, waiting for the end.

*

I have been awake for nearly five days, my mind only resting for a few hours before being interrupted by your presence. I am in my hospital bed, 2:30 a.m. My morphine drip was elevated today in hopes that I could possibly shove food or water down my swollen, throbbing throat. I see you at the end of my bed, cocking your head when I wake suddenly.
I wonder if you are here to take me to euphoria; take me to an afterlife. With every "Code Blue" I hear in my haunted dreams, I think I hear you calling me, my heart racing and breath slowing. Why do you keep waking me? I don't know whether you are good or evil; whether you are rooting for my survival or just toying with your food before devouring me. Instead, I just take in your grand

stature at the end of the bed, the shadow you cast upon me.

I have never seen someone so dark, your silhouette easily distinguishable in the shadows cast by the moon. Tonight, you first appear as a smiling face beside my bed, mocking me as I shove you into the closet. Are you mocking me or is this a sign that I will one day return to the happy girl I once was? I only see you for a moment longer before you stride out of the room, down the hallway, taking your next victim.

third time's a charm

hello, not so nice to see ya
are you afraid?
such a sad and lonely creature
only one to blame

no more flames
juice everyday
hoping the cancer
just goes away

searching for the cure
forget who you were
for now
you are a warrior

denial

try my hardest
to diminish the stress
trying to focus on others' problems
never enough

try my hardest
to clean the house all night
trying to ignore dark thoughts, sadness, anger
never enough

try my hardest
to reinvent myself
new clothes, new name, new hair, new everything
never enough

try my hardest
to run from my anxiety
television, movies, video games
never enough

try my hardest
to forget that tomorrow, my life will change
try to forget i have cancer!
try to diminish the pain

never enough

shipwreck

a ship floats off track
and an inevitable shipwreck follows
we can dwell on the old, broken ship
or we can build a new one
start again

the choice is yours

creature

the only memory haunting my troubled mind
isn't even a memory at all
instead, a figment of my imagination
creeping into my dreams

every strand of hair ripped from her scalp
skin blotchy and scratched; thin scars running up her long neck finally meeting a skull
bones the colour of the overcast skies ahead

stop chasing me, you vile creature!

i run until my lungs collapse
legs barely able to keep me up
the skeleton's hand grasping my shoulders
turning me to look at her face
shocked to see beautiful navy eyes
framed by long lashes

she walks away, a black cloak trailing behind her
leaving me attached to a metal tree;
rooted to the spot as they pump me full of
poison and potions to make the pain go away

and ever...
so...
slowly...

old man next door

hello, the angels greet ya
you found your way
no longer a helpless, lonely creature
no more clouds of grey

you lost your brain,
you lost your way
on a very sad,
and lonely day

it was all a blur,
lots of tears, i'm sure
another fallen
warrior

the world outside

always waiting for
the day
i can leave the nest

one day i will fly
someday
just not today

blue bird

pretty little blue bird
chirps her happy tunes
can't wait to finally rest
as she flies into the room

pretty little blue bird
brightening our day
fluttering her wings
brings out her games to play

pretty little blue bird
always sending love
putting smiles on our faces
always good for a long hug

pretty little blue bird
has to hit the road
already missing her
ask for a text when she gets home

pretty little blue bird
kicks her feet up, time to rest
for the pretty little blue bird
is the absolute best

medical martyrs

the world may not see it,
but what you have endured,
the agony and depression,
anxiety and misery,
was worth it.

for now, so many others won't.

scars

these scars are a reminder
of the pain you once felt
the battles you powered through.
today is another day you are living:
healthy, happy and thriving.
you've worked so hard to continue to live.

make the most of it.

smallz

you returned to remind me that there is light at the end of the tunnel. We gazed at the stars that night; a new beginning, a new era. With you, I began to gain confidence not only in myself but, in people. I hopped in your white Mazda and you led me away from the dark cloud, showing me beauty I had never imagined to see.

ESCAPE

Riding down the coast, Gill and I listened to Brand New, taking in the angry sea foaming at the shore line, the gray skies spitting rain on our windshield, the mountains looming, their grand demeanor exaggerated by the shadows they cast on one another. The tarmac was slick as we drove down the winding roads. Rain tapped on the sun roof, the surrounding emerald forest glistening from the precipitation.

I thought less of the moments spent lying on the bathroom floor, wondering if possibly I could escape the inevitable end, tears inked with mascara, dripping in the same pitter patter tones. I thought less of the many days I spent staring out the clouded windows from my hospital bed, silently begging for the day in which I would no longer have to be tied down by disease. Slowly, the thoughts of my own demise were challenged by the fleeting feeling of freedom. It was as if with every mile we drove, and each sad melody that played through the speakers, a piece of that pain was being washed away with the rain. I was mopping up the white ceramic tiles, slowly but steadily with every fiber of my being. I was cleaning up the chaos the hardships of the past had left. Their essence still lingered but no longer leeched off every bit of my being until I was simply dried up and left with only the toxicity.

The coast soon turned into miles of dense forest. The gentle giants swayed with every drop of rain that fell on their branches. We slowly tiptoed into the thick woods, beautiful red trunks extenuated by the vibrant greens of the rainforest floor, ferns and mosses all at their brightest. Above, the trees created a canopy, small clearings appearing every so often, allowing a break in the shadows each giant cast on the sparkling cement. Standing amongst these elders that had experienced centuries of life, decades of hardships, years of watching as some decompose into the earth to be born again enticed unexplainable calm that flooded through me.

Perhaps I was like one of these giants. I had seen Death just as these goliaths had; experienced the wrath of tremendous storms and downpours, coming out strong all the same. I had fallen and decomposed into the earth, sprouting from the decaying roots of my past, feeding off the liveliness of my own freedom. It was as though I was walking amongst a form of life that maybe could understand me, judge me not by the accomplishments of my short life but by my own liveliness, resilience and character.

I walked up to more than one of the Redwoods, wrapping my arms around its wide trunk, breathing in the dewy scents the rain left on her weathered skin. Life seeped through every pore of the grand being, creatures big and small finding protection and comfort in the giant's arms and within its heart. Yes, there was Death but she seemed so miniscule in that moment, life surrounding us at every angle, overpowering the dark entities of the past. Instead of leeching onto my life, the hike provoked a greater appreciation for its beauty. The sensation of the cool rain hit my skin and reminded me that I was present in a world that saw me just as I was seeing it.

With every breath the wind drew, the forest whispered wise words to us, indistinguishable but comforting all the same. I jumped onto one of the fallen trees, walking down its back to the very edge of its being. I could only smile looking out into the woods around us, and felt peace flood through my veins. At that moment, I finally felt alive.

home

when i say goodbye
sprinkle my ashes amongst the giants
take part of me to the gods

let me float into
the west coast
the pacific ocean
fly at the highest peaks
into the night

bathe in the sunshine
soak up the rays of
vibrant, different cultures
dance to the beats under
city lights

stumble along as we reach the
bottom of the canyon
sing with the spirits
of the navajo

mamma, i'm coming home
just not the same girl that left you a month or so ago
sunshine, i've grown.
i know; it's hard to realize
hon, i'm doing just fine

give me the road,
the open sea, the forestry, the cacti,
oh! give me it all!
finally free, finally home

stargaze at midnight
let the fire ignite our
every thought
chill out to dylan
sing at the top of our lungs

feed our every desire
a taste of psychedelic
joy and laughter
wake up, repeat
we have done it all

darling, keep on smiling
we're so
young and wild and
frightening
keeping it weird
old souls

blue skies, rainy days
we've seen it all
oh, my friend
we have done it all

getting high off life
freedom

mamma, i'm coming home
just not the same girl that left you a month or so ago
sunshine, i've grown.
i know; it's hard to realize
hon, i'm doing just fine

give me the road,
the open sea, the forestry, the cacti,
oh! give me it all!
finally free, finally home

coffee

tiny windows illuminate the shadows of people
getting ready to put on their happy faces
sleepy eyes awakening to show
a spectrum of colour
vibrant, bright

the house is quiet but,
the world outside presents a messily conducted orchestra
a reminder that we are
never alone.

gratitude

if you can rest at the end of the day; with no regrets, a full belly and a roof over your head, you've got a pretty great life.

be grateful

storm is coming

walk, walk, walk
keep going strong
rest; let the others pass
before we move along

walk, walk, walk
keep going strong
cloudy skies ahead
but we stumble along

walk, walk, walk,
we trip, we fall
get to shelter, my dear!
run, walk, crawl!

a storm is coming.

DOWN THE RABBIT HOLE

I met a man waiting to get an x-ray. It was only briefly before he went through the white doors, his hospital robe trailing behind him. The sign above the door ignites into a bright, red word:

X-RAY.

A woman sat beside me- I assumed she was his daughter. We waited patiently, at first in silence. It's tricky to know when to speak these days, especially in a place such as this. Do you ask questions? Do you compliment someone in order to instigate some sort of conversation? Or do you just stare into space silently?

I decide to break the ice and ask for his name. The woman accompanying him replied with a smile. "Socrates. In Greek culture, the son carries on the father's name so it will not be forgotten."

Socrates: the man who chose death knowing he could no longer ask why. Looking around the room, every patient - including myself- was there to try to find answers. WHAT is making us sick? WHAT is the solution? Never WHY are we sick in the first place?

You begin to wonder: are we ignorant to everything happening inside us because of the overload of information? Or were we just choosing to ignore it?

Had we come full circle? Will Socrates, the first to ask 'why?' survive?

Please forgive me for being blunt when I say philosophy has died and that is a very sad thing.

If we all questioned WHY we are doing the things we are - whether that be within our communities, countries whatever - maybe then we could actually solve the issues affecting billions of us; sharing not just basic things like food and water but knowledge and access for one to express their life's wish.

Life has been swapped for this mindless game where you are born into privilege or have some kind of disadvantage you have no control over.

When did we lose our morality? When did we start accepting the injustice that is very much alive in the "New World"?

unexpected diagnosis

hello, not so nice to see ya
are you afraid?
such a fragile, confused creature
no one to blame

you lost your brain
along the way
just another cold
and boring day

searching for the cure
forget who you were
it's time to beat this
young warrior

darkness

hello, darkness, you found me
hoping that happiness is just hiding
hoping that one day i'll see
the light at the end of the tunnel

life is no fairytale.

emergency!!!! (we f***** up)

trip to the general
pain is inevitable
give me some fetynal
just need fucking FETYNAL

this feeling's incredible
this high is exceptional
help me forget it all
just give me some -

swell

what will fix her?
more water!

going in (not out) but
more water!

she's gained 20 lbs (still)
more water!

puffy as hell (who cares!)
she needs

more water!
more water!
more water!

psychosis

i promise i'll do whatever
insanity is fine just
please plEASE (the pain)
PLEASE!!!!!
don't let me die

hello...
Death
(smile big, ry, she might get mad!!!)
you aren't here to take me
are you...
?!?!?!

tall hooded figure at the end of my bed
shakes her head
tyrant smiles
"no,
not just yet
i'm here to prepare you for
the test."

the image of a noose around
my neck comforts me;
mind wanders into the
deepest,
darkest thoughts;
try not to take the
easiest
way out

DeTh returns with tasks
extreme but
do as she says

"rub shit all over your body
rip those tubes from your veins
listen to what i say or
you
will
fail
!!!"

!!!!!!!!!
OKAY OKAY OKAY
I WILL
DO IT
are they watching???
pull -

NO NO STOP
STTTOOOOOPPPP
DON'T
I WILL
FAIL
DON'T
TIE
ME DOWN

*AHHHHHHHHHH
!!!!!!!!*

NO NURSE
I DONT WANT TO BE ON
THIS
REALITY
SHOW
PLEASE

LET ME GO!
LET Me go
let
me…

nightmares!
nightmares!
wake UP!

sob sob sob
what else?!!!?!
sob sob sob
what more can i do?!?!?!

Death laughs
HAHAHAAAA
hahahahaha
ENDURE THE PAIN
STUDY
STUDY
STUDY

am i passing
?!?!?!
DEATHHHHH
AM
I
PASS-
ING?!?!?!

WHEREare you? it's
been
DAYS
i know you can hear me
i know you're watching
am i passing???
AM
I
PASSING??????????

HELLO
HELLO
!?!?!?!?!?!

she's left the classroom for good
sigh of relief
i must have passed
passed the test passed the test
hooray hooray
!!!!!!!!!!!

pump pump pump
let the needles
pump pump pump
make me strong
pump pump pump
nurse leaves the room
just a second -

my face feels
weeeeiiirrrddddd
snapshot and -

UH OH
NO NO NO
WHY
SO PUFFY
WHAT HAVE YOU -

I CAN'T SEE
I CAN'T SEE
HELP ME HELP ME
!!!!!!!!!!!!!!!!!!!!!!!!!!

RING RING RING
CODE BLUE
!!!!!!!
RING RING RING
CODE BLUE
!!!!!
RING RING RING
CODE BLUE
!!!

PLEASE PLEASE
HELP ME!!
HELP ME!!!!

eyes roll
can't stop i can't stop
shaking and
shaking and
shaking

the room begins to change
enveloped by darkness until
fiery candles light up by themselves
Death entering the room once more…

"it's time for the final
it's time for…"

the test.

rotting away in my own toxicity,
worried eyes constantly staring,
a deep sleep lasting minutes, hours, days
trapped

a fat cat stands at the starting line
more confident than i,
gun is raised,
BANG!
the test begins.

running but can not escape
terrified of the unknown
demons slamming doors shut
looking ahead running as fast as i can
anticipating the next "bang!"

fall to the hard stone out of breath,
the fat cat looks down at me,
laughing as he runs ahead:

give up, kid!
you will never beat me!
you will never win!

gripping to the last bit of belief in myself
close my eyes and
remember:

*regardless of the outcome
there will be no regrets if you truly did your best.
don't give up.*

get up on my feet and instead of rushing forward
i turn around and realize the thing slamming the doors
shut are not demons at all

instead, wind blowing through
a large window
beside it,
an old wooden door

walk towards them
take a deep breathe
turn the knob

open the door.

a glimpse of euphoria

an uncomfortable pathway leads to paradise
needles change to sand
flames to flowers
stones to shells
grey to blue
pure bliss

should i stay?

pink hat sits on the beach
blue heron flies over the sea
patiently waiting for me to put it on
waiting to take me home

hop on her back
trusting familiar brown eyes
one more glimpse of paradise
as she flies us
past gold gates
back to life

the consequence of overindulgence

the fat cat runs across hot stones
breathes heavily as he reaches the finish line
impatiently waiting for his trophy.

what is my prize?

before gold gates stands Death
greeting the fat cat with open arms
holding him tight
whispering

"good luck…
how you lived will help me decide…"
eyes changing from blue to red
not a single angel in sight

her eyes open angrily
remaining a fiery red
"do you ever think of all the people you hurt?
all the horrible things you've said?

"think of all the bombs you dropped?
all the children you left for dead?
was the money really worth it?
all the lies and hate you spread?

"do you even consider the world you left behind?
the mother you left to rot, to die;
the mother so desperately trying to survive
the mother starving, the one you selfishly deprived?"

the fat cat looks down
as gold gates turn to flames
a smile emerging onto
Death's bitter face

"it's time to say goodbye."

back to reality

gold gates to closed doors
fluffy clouds to white walls
euphoria to…

where am i?

the heron was gone
where was the pink hat?
what happened to the fat cat?

where am i?

can't move much
so instead, look down
at a familiar green gown

where am i?

glance around the room
beside me stands a metal tree,
pumping a magic potion into me

where am i?

can't ask my questions
no longer have the ability to speak
no longer have the ability to critique

what's happening?

mute

"you know,
she understands everything you're saying, right?
she just can't talk."

big pharma

feel him pumping through my veins,
a cure-all for madness,
the one that takes
the pain away
not so alone when you say his name,
a type of feeling i can't tame

so let me...

follow the white rabbit down the hole
that Alice once went,
fly with dragons in the sky
dance in my green gown,
just a little more
just try to forget
this little pill got me so high...
oh my...

darling, remove me from this life,
your hands they grip my arm so tightly
no honey, can't let you,
just want to inject you
can't let you become my world
but i guess in this prison, this tiny cell

i'll let myself...

follow the white rabbit down the hole
that Alice once went,
fly with dragons in disguise,
hopping from cloud to cloud,
falling down too fast,
not able to soar so high

just call up big pharma,
i'll be just fine

seizure (i'm awake!)

mind racing
shutting down
body shaking
electricity
pulsing
through
my
body
can't
move
(please let me move!)
can't
stop
please
let it -

anxiety

i am constantly at war with my mind
constantly doubting myself
my cries are useless, unheard.
here i stand:
broken.
sick.
unstable.

questioning
did i say the right thing? was it at the right time?
what does the person i am speaking to think of my unique perspective; my strange sense of humor; my striking appearance?

questioning
will i make it to true adulthood?
will this disease take me? or will my mind force me into Death's arms?
will i ever be out of range from my mother's worried gaze?

questioning
when will i stop being the problem?
when will this illness finally leave me alone?

rise up from all of these negative thoughts,
inhale deeply.
1, 2, 3, 4, 5, 6, 7, 8…
release

ying yang

even in the coldest days
light shines through
maybe not as bright but,
enough to
illuminate the overcast skies above

addiction

no longer do i need to follow a white rabbit for a short glimpse of wonderland.
the steady hum of the metal tree that stood beside me seems like a faraway dream
i may be a bird with damaged wings but slowly,
i am learning to fly.

walk in the park

we focus on the rain as it magnifies the trees' creation
a canopy of green - everywhere is green!
look up at an umbrella of tiny green leaves
look down to a carpet of green moss
holes revealing sticks and stones
The Elders' long legs peeking out
every so often

POST FIVE
is this the top?
is this the lookout?
no, not yet - still rocky roads ahead
the hills becoming steeper
the sky becoming brighter as grey clouds fly away

stop! snap a shot!
capture the tree with the crooked spine
as i look at its imperfections - strange yet beautiful
i wonder
why do we strive for perfection?
carry on

higher, higher, higher
let strangers passby
"Hello! Bonjour! Hola!"
just a smile,
no reply
that was enough.

"keep going - i see the lookout!"
we reach the top,
rewarded with a panoramic masterpiece
the water below shines a dark blue,
the forest an emerald green
canoes and kayaks snaking between islands

mom and i stand there smiling,
breathing in the fresh air;
listening to the wind whisper her sweet songs;
taking in the familiar sights
of the first place i truly felt myself

we snap one more picture before heading back
my eyes taking in the final steps of the hike
the end of the trail
i look at mom and smile
wrapping my arms around her,
squeezing her tight

green

with you
everything is enjoyable
feeling energized and excited
instead of focusing on the trip to union station
or the long subway ride,
the large crowds, insane beats
flashing lights
bright and green
is all i see

with you
everything is captivating
electrifying, vibrant
instead of focusing on grey skies
or cold, rainy days
green grass, green leaves
the needles on evergreens
is all i see

with you
everything is painless
feel more motivated to push forward
instead of focusing on the drugs pumping through my veins,
or the long, white hallways
the change from STOP to GO
red to green
is all i see

with you
everything is peaceful
feeling relaxed and care-free
instead of focusing on the breathtaking sunset
or the calm waves, cool breeze
looking at you,
green
is all i see

thunder

the storm isn't over
a flash of light and then
boom

THE FINAL BATTLE

Why? That was the question. We knew something was wrong. I had gone from being full of energy to helplessly tired. It reminded me of the first battle but this time, I knew.

Everyday it became harder. We waited until it was confirmed: the cancer was back but this time, it was worse. Fluid had wrapped itself around my brain and the question we asked was why? Had the cancer finally taken over? Was it brain cancer?

We did tests, scans, you name it. Everyone thought we were going to get the confirmation from a biopsy. My skull was drilled and the fluid was taken. We waited. We were so scared.

Luckily, the cancer hadn't taken over. The biopsy was negative. My brain wasn't sick; just hurt. But the question still remained: why?

I was going insane and it was getting worse and worse. I heard the demons all day now disguising themselves as nurses screaming. "Bitch! Whore! Slut!" It was all a figment of my imagination but it felt so real.

Finally, my brain began to heal and it was time to kill the cancer remaining in my abdomen. After the holidays, I would begin chemo prepping for another stem cell transplant from someone else's cells. I wasn't scared - I had done this before, I could do it again. Things became worse. The day after my birthday, I was back on C4. I don't remember much so to this day I ask the question: Why?

When I was strong enough, we proceeded with the first round of chemotherapy. Then it happened. I was sent to the ICU, going crazy at first then not breathing without the assistance of a ventilator. Black tar was removed from my lungs, and finally, I was sent back to C4. The ten days I had spent downstairs had made me so weak.

But I couldn't give up. Everyone had worked so hard to keep me alive. I couldn't let them down. So everyday, I worked harder. Everyday, I got stronger. After the next round of chemo, I was sent home.

The battle wasn't over but I knew it would be soon.

the final diagnosis

hello, you crazy creature
the one screaming horrible names
unsure if you even had a future
for you were going insane

was this just a dream
or was it true?
was it just the question
haunting you?

searching for a cure
forget who you were
this is the final battle
young warrior

voices

BITCH!
hearing voices
SLUT!
no one is screaming
WHORE!
it's all in my head

the devil within

angels watching from glass windows
sneaking in to pump out
the tar inside my lungs

open my eyes and meet hers
angry, navy eyes
Death tossing the demons

down the tunnel
down the hole
back to hell

fight

you have worked so hard
everyday gaining more strength
starting to understand this is it
the final battle
the end of the war.

to all the nurses

you are the angels sent to protect us from
the disgusting illness trying to take us down
the saviours that help us
move toward a better life

thank you.

heron

you allow me to soar but always keep me grounded
more satisfied by giggles, jokes, smiles, and laughs
than constant arguments, useless banter.

they say before you die,
before you move on to whatever comes next,
your life plays before your eyes

i, for one, would much rather watch
a long, dreamy screening of a life full of exciting memories
than a series of distressing ones depicting wasted, miserable moments.

wouldn't you?

the journey

even though the climb uphill is hard,
the view from the top is spectacular
entices a feeling of accomplishment
inspires you to move forward
to take the next step

well worth it

fresh start

clear the page.
today marks a new chapter
for today,
you can flush all the toxic waste down the drain
free yourself from the chains that have held you down
for so long.
it is not easy to break loose from the metal tree that has
rooted you to the spot
for **so** long.
but, my friend, the day has come!
no more tears! no more pain!
finally, young warrior,
so strong, so brave...

you are free.

DEAR DEATH

You had never been taught how to truly love; forgotten so much of your lonely life. I won't ever fully forget you, never lied when I said I loved you; allowed your sadness to project itself onto me, leaving me cold but wanting more.

Unfortunately, you fall out of love. You start to care about your own depression, your own life, your own journey. Almost dying does that to you, being so close to its dark doors, seeing the vacancy sign shining bright, the word "NO" flickering ever so often, preparing for its next victim. I have spent endless time sitting in a different kind of prison, alone with my thoughts but realizing the life I want to live. I am happy and really hope you are too.

I'll see you when it's time to depart, when I'm ready to follow you into the darkness. I'll never forget you.

See you in euphoria.

Ryan

ACKNOWLEDGEMENTS

I'd really like to thank everyone who's stuck through this battle with me: my wonderful family, my awesome friends, the nurses, Dr. Foley, and Alex. Most of all, I want to thank my mom.

Mom, I really wouldn't be here without you. You've stuck through this, researching everything to try to make this battle easier, trying to find me a cure. You've always been my shoulder to cry on, the one who took a break from your own life just to make sure I could live mine. You have no idea how grateful I am to have a mother like you; strong, intelligent, sympathetic, and giving. I love you more than anything.

ABOUT THE AUTHOR

Ryan Gardner is a twenty-seven-year-old woman who has been battling Hodgkin's lymphoma since she was just sixteen. She's overcome five battles, having to deal with epilepsy, post-traumatic stress, psychosis, addiction and even a coma. She still came out strong.

Today, Ryan's goal is to help others fight their battles with cancer. She one day wishes to create a retreat for these warriors to give them a day to get away from the hardships and relax. She also hopes to be able to donate money to cancer research and SickKids Hospital.

CPSIA information can be obtained
at www.ICGtesting.com
Printed in the USA
LVHW080312281021
701773LV00008B/272/J

9 780228 860433